THE CALM BEFORE THE SALE

CALM- DRIVEN SELLING SECRETS
OF A SUCCESSFUL CAR SALESPERSON

KATIA TIKHONRAVOVA & SHAHEED KHAN

Copyright © 2015 by Corporation Clinic, Inc.

All rights reserved. No part of this publication may be reproduced, distributed, or transmitted in any form or by any means, or stored in a database or retrieval system, including scanning, photocopying, or otherwise without the prior written permission of the copyright holder.

www.CorporationClinic.com

First Printing, 2015

ISBN 978-1-505-24434-2

Printed in the United States of America

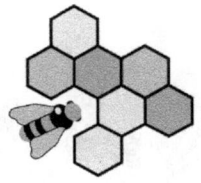

Copration Clinic
NOURISHING THE WORK ENVIRONMENT

Corporation Clinic
provides systemic counseling, mediation,
training and coaching services
that helps individuals and organizations
to increase job satisfaction

Visit **www.CorporationClinic.com**
www.FaceBook.com/CorporationClinic
e-mail office@corporationclinic.com
or call 954.253.2720 or 965.654.1656
to schedule an individual coaching session
or group training.

CONTENTS

Introduction   5

PART I

ONE: What a Spider Can Learn From a Bee   6
TWO: The Car Business   12
THREE: Set a Goal   15
FOUR: From Selling To Sold   21
FIVE: This Is My Specialty   28
SIX: Networking: A Bee Style   38

PART II

SEVEN: The Law of Anxiety   44
EIGHT: #1 Car Salesperson's Mistake   62
NINE: The Law of Calmness   68
TEN: The Calm-Driven Sale   78

PART III

ELEVEN: Traditional vs. Calm-Driven Selling   89
TWELVE: Keep Your Customers Close and Your Coworkers Closer   93
THIRTEEN: Calm-Driven Customer Satisfaction Index (CSI)   100

About the Authors   104

INTRODUCTION

This book is a manual and addition to trainings in Calm-Driven Selling for car salespeople who want to love their job again, make more money, and understand their customers better. This manual covers a lot of material and should be read slowly.

Part I of the Calm-Driven Selling manual helps car salespeople to create a road map to success and shares some business generating tips and techniques of successful Calm-Driven salespeople. Do not skip Part II of this book. This part goes over fundamental concepts of Calm-Driven Selling. Part III goes over benefits that come from Calm-Driven Selling. Read all chapters multiple times.

This book aims to bring you new ideas, reawaken your passion, and create lasting results in your car sales career.

PART I

CHAPTER 1

WHAT A SPIDER CAN LEARN FROM A BEE

A Spider

A spider is a powerful, smart, patient, and dangerous insect. Spiders create a web for hunting, storage, and living. This web is a death sentence for many insects. The success and survival of the spider becomes dependent on how large, popular, and strong the web is. A web can cover a large territory and bring a lot of prey to its predator. Many are destroyed before they are finished.

All webs start with one line of silk. A spider patiently and diligently works step by step, line by line, to create his kingdom. After the web is built, a spider waits for the food to arrive on its platter. Patience becomes the most important ability of the spider.

Some car salespeople are like those powerful, smart, patient, and dangerous spiders. They build their knowledge like a web, step by step in their area of expertise until they become untouchable. They are masters of product knowledge, paperwork, walk-around, negotiation, closing, and other aspects of the car sales business. No matter what type of situation may arise, they know what steps to take to get the customer to take a delivery. Customers do not leave the dealership without a car if they meet this salesperson.

The problem of the spider's business life is that the success of the hunting will strictly depend on the size and popularity of the web. Even though a Spider Car Salesperson is very confident in the product they present and the layers of the business they are in, this car salesperson depends on the customer coming to them. Sometimes spiders eat daily, however sometimes they go without food for months. In the same way, a car salespeople can close a few deals in one day, while sometimes be in a "negative" for a few months in a row because this business structure is not consistent.

The other problem of the Spider Car Salesperson is the lack of flexibility. The salesperson can feel stuck in the same place. The thought that the grass is greener on other side comes to us in those moments. This leads us into making drastic and irrational decisions. In addition, not all of us are patient like a spider and we leave the web before the customer visits us and our hunger is taken care of. The most dangerous mistake of the Spider Car Salesperson is in treating customers like victims and taking life out of them as soon as they come our way. The customers who do not enjoy the sales process, realize that they were lied to, are insulted or mistreated, will not come back to buy their next car from the same salesperson or refer their friends and family to them.

A Honeybee

On the other hand, there is the Honeybee Car Salesperson. Honeybees go outside their home environment in search of nectar. This is what some car salespeople do. They network and ask for referrals, send emails and cards, call previous customers, create social media pages, and even deliver and complete the paperwork in the comfort of the customer's home instead of the dealership. Honeybee Car Salespeople go outside their comfort zone, their dealership walls, in search for new business opportunities.

The honeybees fly the same territory. They visit the same flower fields every day of their adult lives and those flowers continue to award them with more nectar. In comparison with the Spider Car Salesperson who takes life out of the customers by making the most money on that customer, the Honeybee

Car Salesperson takes care of the customer like a bee takes care of the flower. The flower, in return, pays its respect by providing more nectar the next time. Customers return for business to the caring car salesperson and refer their friends and family to him or her. This creates a stronger customer base.

The honeybees work hard and it pays off. The Honeybee Car Salespeople keep going outside to get a sale and they work the same customer base. If working hard like a bee does not sound as attractive as sitting on a web and just waiting for a victim, think about the benefits that consistency can bring. A single bee colony can produce more than 100 pounds of extra honey. Extra, meaning after you paid all your bills.

The Difference

Honeybee Car Salespeople are successful because they come from the place of giving, not receiving. They work in terms of trust, friendship, and respect, not only with customer but other "bees" as well. Honeybee Car Salespeople have equal and respectful relationships with other salespeople, managers, finance managers, service writers, insurance writers, and other professionals in a field. They ask for referrals, split deals, teach, and support each other. Spider Car Salespeople, however, feel threatened by the existence of another salesperson on the same sales floor.

Many car salespeople are trained to be spiders. They view another salesperson's success as their own failure. This leads to an aggressive and competitive environment, which could be a good thing until spiders become more focused on their competitors than their prey. The Honeybee Car Salesperson views another salesperson's success as an opportunity to learn new skills from their colleagues, more referrals, and more income to the dealership, which could lead to more "spiffs" and income opportunities. Those bees work together to make the colony stronger, creating a supportive and encouraging work environment.

We Train Honeybees

When a bee colony is under a threat, the level of anxiety of each honeybee goes up. They start flying faster, making more noise, and stay focused on a predator instead of producing honey. This is the way the Law of Anxiety works. In cases of high intensity, our anxiety increases, forcing us to react in a different way from our calm state. A Honey Bee Car Salesperson understands natural human relations, the Law of Anxiety, and the Law of Calmness. This knowledge helps them not react to the conflict and view the situation from a distance.

Hardworking honeybees are masters of Calm-Driven functioning. Operating under the Law of Calmness allows honeybees to come from the place of giving and, in return, constantly receiving nectar from their customers. A Honeybee Car Salesperson understands and takes advantage of the Law of Calmness every day. They are always on the go but calm internally. Honeybees function with a goal and purpose, and the success of each individual honeybee helps maintain the success of the colony.

The Law of Anxiety and the Law of Calmness help sales professionals understand customers' behaviors while increasing productivity and job satisfaction. In order to understand the magic of the Law of Anxiety and the Law of Calmness, salespeople must first understand themselves. For this reason, the first part of this book helps you set goals and follow a plan.

Chapter 2

THE CAR BUSINESS

The car business is one of the most rewarding, exciting, and satisfying careers in the sales industry. Selling cars is one of the highest paying jobs, and it does not require a college education. You can make a good living without owing a fortune in college debt. It allows your natural sales talents to shine and for you to take full advantage of its financial and other rewards. The success of a car salesperson does not depend on age, race, gender, sexual orientation, or family inheritance. Instead, success depends on a salesperson's persistence, talent, and charisma. In a car business, you can create your own American dream.

> "CAR SALES IS NOT A JOB.
> CAR SALES IS A CAREER."

Car sales is a career, not a job. In the car business, most people are promoted from within. Most presidents of car dealerships were working the sales floor at the beginning of their career with everyone else. If you are the best salesman or saleswoman on a floor, it is only a matter of time before you will be invited to become a closer, sales manager, or finance manager. Experience, practice, some in-house education, and most importantly, your relationships with colleagues and customers will take you to the position and income you want to have. It is up to you whether you prefer to stay at the salesperson level or aim to become a president and run the dealership. In this business, anything is possible. The results depend on you.

Car sales is a captivating, fascinating, and gratifying business. If you find pleasure from working in this business, it is very hard to find the same satisfaction in another field. It is interesting that many car salespeople leave dealerships but they do not leave the car business.

If you are in the car business until you find something else, or because you can get paid minimum wage by sitting outside, waiting on an up, please close this book now. First, because it will be boring to you. Second, because we do not want to share our secrets of success in the car business with someone who will never use them. This book is for men and women who love, appreciate, and want to make the best out of their car sales career. This book is also for men and women who feel burned out from the car business but still have hope that they will shine again.

This book explains the car business from a unique, Calm-Driven Sales view that brings out better relationships with car buyers. Calm-Driven Sales allow salespeople to understand their customers in a more personalized way, leading to an increase in sales, higher customer satisfaction, and increase in repeat business. Understanding how Calm-Driven Sales works will also help salespeople to create better relationships with colleagues, leading to a friendlier, more welcoming, and more supportive environment.

Marriage and family therapists and other mental health professionals knew about Calm-Driven relationships for decades but kept it a secret, sharing it only with academics or clients who could afford their fees. This book combines the best strategies of a salesperson and a marriage and family therapist to explain the magic of Calm-Driven Selling.

Chapter 3

SET A GOAL

> *"Find something you love to do,
> and you'll never work a day in your life"*
> Attributed to Harvey MacKay

Decide for yourself if the car business is for you. Do you love talking to people, completing a sale transaction, and receiving that commission paycheck? The answer to this question does not depend on how many cars you sell. The answer to this question depends on your attitude toward the car business and your place in it.

If nothing about a car business excites you, why are you even in it? You could be a top salesperson in a dealership, but if you hate what you do, you are wasting your life. At the same time, if you are a salesperson who does not sell as many cars as expected, but you love what you do and feel ecstatic every time you sell a car, do what make you feel good. If you love the car business, do not let others discourage you and get you off your game. When you love what you do and you are willing to work hard, you will reach any goal you set for yourself, fulfill your life, and make money.

The first step to success is setting a goal. No one can set the goal for you better than you can. Therefore, this chapter could be written only by you and for you. Take time and answer questions below to set a direction for what you want, why you want it, and how you will achieve it.

What

"I think the biggest disability that we have as a human being is unbelief. Everything starts with a vision and the man without vision dies."
Nick Vujicic

Moving without a goal is surviving. Moving with a goal is living. Stop moving in circles and set a direction for yourself. No matter how unrealistic this goal may sound in the beginning, keep that goal in your mind. Whatever your desire, it will come to you if you want it bad enough. Set a glorious goal for yourself. A goal that will make you wake up with a smile every day. That will bring you enjoyment, fulfill you, and give you an extraordinary life. You are going to reach only what you set for yourself, so make your goal magnificent, astonishing, and glorious. Make your goal big. Ask for a miracle.

Do you want more money? Do you want more recognition and respect? Do you want better relationships? What is it that you want from your life? What is it that you need?

Write your goal here:

_____

_____

_____

_____

_____

_____

Results

> *"The Man who says he can,*
> *and the man who says he can not…*
> *Are both correct."*
> Attributed to Confucius

Imagine you already achieved your goal. What did it bring into your life? How is your life different now after you achieved this goal? What do you have now that you did not have before?

Answer at least one question:

_____

_____

_____

_____

_____

_____

_____

_____

_____

_____

Why

You will not work hard, climb over the obstacles, and achieve your goal unless you know why you are doing it. On a day when nothing seems to work, what will push you to keep going? On a day when your plan B was worse than plan A, what will tell you let's do it again, or let's try something different? On that day, it will be easy to give up unless you know why you keep working.

Why do you want to achieve this goal? Why will you work hard, learn, and sweat every day to reach your desire?

Your answer:

_____

_____

_____

_____

_____

_____

_____

_____

_____

How

Spiders hope and pray for the prey come to them. This hope is strong enough for them to believe that their needs would be fulfilled. This hope provides them with patience and persistence. Without hope, you lose the reason to keep doing what you are doing. Entitlement is a fool's hope. That is where the problem for many car salespeople comes in. Nobody is entitled to anything. Spiders are not entitled to anything. Work for what you want.

Knowing what you want, what it will give you, and why you want it will awaken your determination. This will help you keep moving no matter how many rocks could block your way. The stronger your determination is, the stronger your chances to reach your goal. Honey Bee Salespeople are determined. They are motivated to burn that energy, get up, and move. Honey Bee Salespeople not only want to get it done, they want to get it done now.

> *"You can't climb the ladder of success with your hands in your pockets"*
> Arnold Schwarzenegger

People who find the answers to what, why, and how the easiest are people whose goal is going after a goal. Those people love what they do. For them, it is not about getting things done to achieve a goal but about how to make process even more enjoyable, fun, and productive.

Now that you know what you want, what it will give you, and why you want it, let's talk about how you will get there. By this point, you should be able to tell if your answers have anything to do with the car business or not. If the car business is not your passion, ask yourself what is and do that, but do not stay in the car business. People who love to sell cars will continue to love selling cars, making money, and meeting new people. They will get more successful, knowledgeable, and satisfied with what they are doing as time goes by. Some of them will keep a salesperson position while others will get a promotion and become managers or even run their own dealership. For them, it will not be about the position, it will be about enjoying what they do.

Before reading about tools on how to achieve success in the car business, take your time and write your own ideas about how to reach your goal.

How to achieve your goal:

_____

_____

_____

_____

_____

_____

_____

_____

Chapter 4

FROM SELLING TO SOLD

> *"Small deeds done are better than great deeds planned"*
> Peter Marshall

Congratulations on setting your goal. Now that your goal is set, you have a vision, and determination. There is nothing left but to act. Do not procrastinate. Do it now. Do not stop yourself if your vision is not 100% complete. Action will bring you to a clearer goal. There is no productivity in contemplating doing something. Only by doing what you set up to be doing will you know what you need to do next. Just keep moving toward your goal. The principle of equifinality will help you achieve what you set for yourself.

> **"THERE IS NO PRODUCTIVITY IN CONTEMPLATING DOING SOMETHING. DO IT."**

Equifinality is a principle stating that there are multiple ways of reaching the end state. This means you may reach your goal in different ways. For example, a customer could lease a car or the same customer could buy the same car and you could end up with the same commission either way. Same customer, same car, same results, but different ways to get the same result. That is equifinality. The same with your goal. You can work from the same start and achieve the same result by doing different things. Some techniques are better than others. It is up to you to find what works better for you. It is ok to change your approach in how you do things every so often, as long as it will bring you the same result. However, you will never know the better way to do it until you try it.

> "IT IS UP TO YOU TO FIND WHAT WORKS BETTER FOR YOU."

The problem is that sometimes we do not know where to start. In this case, break down your goal into steps. This will make a goal more reachable. It is like losing weight. You do not tell yourself I will lose 30 pounds this year. You say I will lose 2.5 pounds every month for a year (30 pounds/12 months = 2.5 pounds) and you will lose 30 pounds at the end of the year. This way you can follow your progress more easily and stay on track.

One Degree

> *"At 211 degrees, water is hot. At 212 degrees, it boils."*
> Sam Parker and Mac Anderson

In 1724, German physicist Daniel Gabriel Fahrenheit invented the temperature measurement scale. In his measurement scale, Fahrenheit used cool seawater as 0 degrees and average human body temperature as 100 degrees. Any temperature degree became relative to those two measures.

Twenty years later, in search of more precise temperature measurement, Swedish astronomer Andres Celsius invented a temperature measurement scale using purified water. Celsius used the point at which water freezes into ice as 0 degrees, which is 32 degrees Fahrenheit, and the point at which water boils as 100 degrees, which is 212 degrees Fahrenheit.

The difference between 211 and 212 degrees Fahrenheit:

- Microwave coffee is 211 degrees. Starbucks coffee is 212 degrees.
- 211 degree soup is full of bacteria. 212 degree soup kills the vegetative stage of all common microbes, saving millions of lives.
- 211 degree sterilization is still full of bacteria. 212 degree steam sterilization is nontoxic and inexpensive way to keep us safe.

> *"If you change one element in a system, or the relationship between that element and another element, the system as a whole will be affected"*
> Steve de Shazer and Insoo Kim Berg

One extra degree, step, or smile can make a huge difference in your career success. First, divide your goal into measurable steps. A honey bee visits anywhere between 50-100 flowers during one collection trip and every flower is equally important. Your goal can consist out of 212 steps, 100 steps; however, we like 10 steps.

On a scale from 1 to 10, when 10 is the level where your financial, career, or relationship goal is accomplished, and 1 is the situation at its worst, what number would you give to your current progress?

Your answer _____

What will cause that score to go up one level?

Your answer

_____

_____

_____

_____

_____

_____

_____

Do not expect to function at 212 degrees right away. Even a Corvette needs 3.8 seconds to reach 60 mph. Do only the things that you listed for yourself to get to the next level. If you need, break those goals into more steps. When you reach one level higher, ask yourself what needs to happen for this score to go up another level?

> *"You don't set out to build a wall. You don't say 'I'm going to build the biggest, baddest, greatest wall that's ever been built.' You don't start there. You say, 'I'm going to lay this brick as perfectly as a brick can be laid.' You do that every single day. And soon you have a wall."*
> Will Smith

If you experience difficulty to achieve your steps, consider to reevaluate your determination. Measure your hope and motivation. Ask yourself again why you are working so hard. There is no progress without hope and motivation.

Hope

On a scale from 1 to 10, with 1 being a place with absolutely no hope or confidence that your goal will be achieved, and 10 being complete confidence and hopeful, what number would you give to your current hope?

Your answer _____

What will tell you that your score has gone up one level?

Your answer

_____

_____

_____

_____

_____

_____

_____

What number will be high enough for you to work hard to try to change things?

Your answer _____

Motivation

On a scale from 1 to 10, with 1 being no motivation and 10 being a willingness to go any lengths to solve your problem, what number would you give your current motivation?

Your answer _____

What will cause that score to go up one level?

Your answer
_____
_____
_____
_____
_____
_____
_____
_____

What number will be high enough for you to work hard to try change things?

Your answer _____

> *"If you always put limits on everything you do, physical or anything else, it will spread into your work and into your life. There are no limits. There are only plateaus, and you must not stay there, you must go beyond them."*
> Bruce Lee

You will never reach 10. You will find that every time you moved to 9 or 9.5, your goal evolves to even larger success and opportunities. We congratulate you if you reach that level.

Chapter 5

THIS IS MY SPECIALTY

Every cook has a dish that they call their specialty. If you cook, you know how to make your specialty dish taste delicious every time. As time goes by, you get more knowledge and experience. The longer you practice your cooking techniques, the more dishes you call your specialty. However it always starts from that one dish.

Chicken wings and potatoes are Katia's specialty. Most of her family and friends would prefer she make that dish, not because others cannot do the same but because they know it is her specialty and she will provide the results without a hassle. However, when people are craving some steak, no one looks her way. They look at Shaheed because that is his specialty.

People could ask Katia to make some steak but why would they go to her if they know Shaheed can provide better results for what they are asking. This is the same way they would not go to him for chicken wings and potatoes. They are both cooks but their specialties distinguish what orders they will get. That is the rule of specialization in marketing and advertising.

Most successful stores follow the rules of specialization. They specialize in one line of product and become experts in that line. These stores do not sell everything under the sun. They are specialists in a product they sell and focus on that. For example, a professional sunglasses store will not sell meat, and a professional jewelry store will not sell hats. Instead, they will show their customers that they have knowledge and understanding of a specific product and customer's needs. Even large stores that have a large item selection sort them by categories such as gender, colors, seasons, and so on. Pharmacies and groceries stores are great example of specialization in a multiple item store. These stores create aisles that specialize in products their customers are interested in, such as a drinks aisle, vitamins aisle, frozen aisle, and others.

Professionals specialize as well. Lawyers specialize in divorce, bankruptcy, accidents, arbitration, or other aspects of law. Doctors specialize in optometry, spine, psychiatry, and other aspects of health. Dealerships specialize in new and/or used cars, trucks, and SUVs of specific makes and models.

Customers trust leaders and experts more than general providers. Specialization increases customer's confidence in a product or service provided by an individual or a company. It lets customers know that they are dealing with a professional. Customers feel these companies and individuals will understand their needs better, be more familiar with their order, know pros and cons better than they would, provide them with all the options, and help to make wiser choices. Most customers also assume that dealing with individuals or companies that specialize in their need will have a larger variety of products and services specific to what they are looking for.

> "SPECIALIZATION INCREASES CUSTOMER'S CONFIDENCE IN A PRODUCT OR SERVICE PROVIDED BY AN INDIVIDUAL OR A COMPANY."

A Salesperson's Specialty

Car salespeople can and should specialize as well. They already specialize in a product they sell. They make that decision when they come looking for a job at a dealership that is specializing in a specific car make, like Lexus or Ford. The company, not a salesperson, determines what vehicles a company sells. Then, in negotiation with a dealership, a salesperson will be assigned to new cars, used cars, a fleet, the Internet, car services, or even all of the above departments. Depending on a salesperson's knowledge and experience, he or she could have multiple specializations, like a cook who has more specialties as he or she gets more knowledge and experience in a kitchen.

These specializations are car business specific. The problem with this specialization is that it will not make you stand out from other salespeople, which decreases your chances of selling and having committed customers. The specialization car salespeople need for wild success in the car business is relationship specific. Relationship specific specialization will help you focus on a specific group of people who have similar interests with you. Relationship specialization will make you stand out from other salespeople, it will give you more credit, send you more referrals, and help you dominate the market in that field.

> "THE SPECIALIZATION YOU NEED FOR WILD SUCCESS IN THE CAR BUSINESS IS RELATIONSHIP SPECIFIC."

Structuring business around a specific group, like lesbian, gay, bisexual, transgender, and questioning (LGBTQ) communities, is a great relational specialty example. Members, friends, family, and LGBTQ supporters will not buy a car from a car salesperson who is prejudiced toward the LGBTQ community. A high level of discrimination motivates LGBTQ community members, friends, family members, and supporters to look for a professional in the car business who would respect their sexual expression and identity. A salesperson that would not judge two fathers with three children and accommodate two ladies with respect. A member, friend, family, or supporter of the LGBTQ community who knows a car salesperson that markets him or herself as LGBTQ friendly will get many LGBTQ customers to buy a car from him or her.

Working with the LGBTQ community is Shaheed's specialty. He reaches this community via social media, attending community events, and decorating his office with LGBTQ symbols. Most members, family, friends, and LGBTQ supporters prefer to buy and lease from him not because they could not buy from someone else but because they know it is his specialty. With him they can relax, feel safe and welcomed. That is his specialty. What is yours?

When Katia was selling cars, the Russian community was her relational specialty. The ability to speak Russian and English did most of the marketing job for her. The more Russian families she knew, the more Russian families introduced Katia to even more Russian families. She reached this community through Russian and Ukrainian church and social media. That is her specialty. What is yours?

Finding Your Specialty

Finding your own specialty is difficult and fun at the same time. This should be a community that you are called to serve. If you disrespect this community in any way, even internally, your mannerisms will give you away and will backfire faster than you think. Customers will also feel if you are passionate and caring about them and this will pay back ten fold.

Think about what community you hold the most respect for and enjoy being with.

Write your answer:

_____

_____

_____

_____

Now think about your perfect customers. Do they live in a certain area? Work or relax at a certain place? What is their average annual income? What are their traits or hobbies?

Write your answer:

_____

_____

_____

_____

What do you enjoy doing that is similar to the lifestyle of your customers? It could be attending church, gym, strip clubs, or other groups as long as it involves communication with other people.

Write your answer:

_____

_____

_____

_____

With which community do you have the highest contact rate? This is not necessarily a community that you have personal contact with, but maybe your spouse, children, and friends do. This may include your spouse and friend's job or your children's school.

Write your answer:

_____

_____

_____

_____

What do those answers have in common for you? Which community sparks your interest, or which community have you wanted to work with for a long time but have not yet gotten around to? Some of you already know what community you want to focus on. Others will need to take some time. Start with only one community. This will help you to focus your energy more productively and give you better results. One right market community is enough to become the top salesperson in a dealership and even district. However, just like a cook who has multiple specialties, you may find yourself marketing to a few market communities as time passes.

Marketing

Specializing is about knowing what you are selling. Relational Specialization is about knowing to whom you are selling. Marketing is about who knows what you are selling.

The majority of salespeople are Spider Car Salespeople. They do not market. Instead, they sit on a web and wait for their prey to come to them. They are upset that all ups they get from waiting outside in the heat, rain, and cold have came to see a Honeybee Salesperson and complain about slow foot traffic in a dealership.

Spiders who are Honeybee Car Salespeople in training are more creative. These salespeople market to everyone without specializing in customers they are marketing to. This is similar to not marketing at all because marketing to everyone does not make a salesperson different from another salesperson. It does not make you stand out.

It is understandable why salespeople would want to market to everyone. Many salespeople wish for everyone to know that they are selling vehicles and come to buy cars from them. The truth is, you cannot market to everyone. Think, what is it that makes you stand out from another salesperson when you are marketing to everyone? Nothing!

A Honeybee Car Salesperson attracts customers by marketing their services to a specific community. They actively stay in touch and nourish their chosen community. In return, they sell a majority of the vehicles to the members from that community, get referrals, and become recognized as a specialist.

Note that both Spider and Honeybee Car Salespeople are experts in the product they are selling, but only the Honeybee Salesperson is an expert in customer relations. They create their own unique image that draws customers to them because what they offer is different. By specializing, they tell the world that they are professional, that they understand the needs of the population they are working with.

Specializing in customer relations makes it easier to create common ground and trustful and respectful relationships with the community you specialize in. Specialization gives customers more confidence that you care about their needs. Customers see you as a friend instead of a Spider Car Salesperson who would take life out of them.

> "SPECIALIZING
> IS ABOUT KNOWING
> WHAT YOU ARE SELLING.
>
> RELATIONAL SPECIALIZATION
> IS ABOUT KNOWING
> TO WHOM YOU ARE SELLING.
>
> MARKETING
> IS ABOUT WHO KNOWS
> WHAT YOU ARE SELLING."

Specialization does not restrict a Honeybee from selling a vehicle to customers outside the community of his or her specialty. A Honeybee Salesperson sells and leases vehicles to everyone but dominates sales from the community that is his or her specialty.

Attracting Your Community

There are a multiple ways of attracting members from the community, including social media, emailing, attending events, public speaking, and other strategies that have low financial cost. You can get as creative in your marketing as you desire. The main goal is to spark your preferred community's interest. You will be especially successful if you are able to make your community feel special and introduce yourself as a benefit to them.

Let's say your community is college students. You send your flyers to the university, attend their events, and post your specials on Facebook. When you market to them, specify that only they have the privilege of this discount. Customers appreciate and will act on a special that is designed especially for them more than if it is open to anyone. Customers give those promotions more value and urgency when they are specific and these people are privileged to qualify for them. Make sure you follow all your dealership's guidelines and all your postings are approved by the management.

Remember, what you offer is not lower prices or faster cars. You offer relational connection and understanding of the community's needs. For example, if you are working with an elderly community, you may offer to bring a car to their house for a test drive and complete paperwork in the comfort of their home.

What can you give to your community that is unique and will be appreciated by them?

_____

_____

_____

_____

_____

_____

_____

> "FIND YOUR SPECIALIZATION BEFORE ALL CUSTOMERS GO TO A SALESPERSON WHO ALREADY DID."

Chapter 6

NETWORKING: A BEE STYLE

> *"Work smarter, not harder."*
> Allan H. Mogensen

Salespeople have no time to network. After working for six days a week, networking is the last thing that we want to do on our day off, and while we are on the clock, we focus on getting ups, not networking.

The good news is that salespeople are already networking all the time. We meet new people every single day, unless we have been in a dark corner of the web for a very long time. Most of us can easily come up with a list of 200 referral sources that we are working throughout the year. The best thing a Honey Bee Salesperson does is staying in touch with those referral sources. For example, we send cards with birthday wishes, emails with new promotions, and invitations to the events at the dealership.

The goal is to create your referral database with those 200 individuals and make it stronger. The best referrals are customers and professionals in other fields. They are not interested in stealing your customers and they know a lot of people who are looking to buy or lease a vehicle. Take some time and write down 200 people you know who could refer customers to you. This could be your past customers, friends, and different business encounters.

Some of you will create a list of 200 referral sources in a flash, while others will stop at the 5th person. No matter if your list is full or empty, think who else could be your best referral source. To start, make a list of 16 people you do not know, and from whom you could receive a large number of referrals.

For example, here is our list of people we wish to know:

1. Divorce lawyer: Ex-spouses cannot divide a car. We can help with that.

2. Car accident lawyer: You need to drive something after your car was totaled.

3. Bankruptcy attorney: Buy a new car while you still can finance.

4. Mechanic: If you can't fix customer's car, at least refer them to us and get a referral fee.

5. Car insurance agent: They know customers' cars and financial needs.

6. Car appraiser: They appraise the car after the accident.

7. Realtor: Just moved to Florida? Do you need a car too?

8. Owner of the car rental store: Some people rent cars while they are looking for one.

9. Owner of the tire store: They put tires on your customers' cars.

10. High school teacher: They know what families look for in a car for their new driver.

11. Driving school teacher/owner: What do their students drive after graduating?

12. Young Entrepreneur: Make money from home by referring people to us.

13. Banker/Financial Consultant/Credit Union Representative: Some customers apply for a car loan before walking into your dealership.

14. Chiropractor/Doctor: A person your customer trusts.

15. Therapist/Social worker: They know your customer struggles.

16. Neighbor: They know people too.

Create your own list here. Write down people you do not yet know:

1 _____

2 _____

3 _____

4 _____

5 _____

6 _____

7 _____

8 _____

9 _____

10 _____

11 _____

12 _____

13 _____

14 _____

15 _____

16 _____

Great job!

Spend 5-10 min a day for 4 days out of the week and make new contacts with people from this list. With their help, you can sell more than 200 cars a year.

This is how it works:

- Car salespeople work 6 days a week. However, you will network for only 4 days out the week. The other 2 days are money making weekend days. 4 weeks with 4 networking days will equal 16 new referral contacts.

- 16 new network contacts must stay contacts. If you build relationships with them, move them to your 200 list. Fill the spaces on your list of 16 with new names.

- The 4 days a week and 50 weeks (52 weeks, minus 2 vacation weeks) in a year adds up to 200 new contacts a year.

- Some network contacts will never refer a customer to you while others will refer more than 20 a year. To keep it simple, let's say each referral gives you 1 sale a year. This will equal out to 200 new car sales a year. Would your check improve from this simple Honey Bee Car Salesperson strategy?

Find those new networking contacts on social media, like Facebook, LinkedIn, and Twitter. Google their services and look up their websites. Stop by their office or shop. Send them email, and use other creative ways to get in touch. Tell those new contacts about you, your services, and referral fee. Ask them for a referral and make sure you pay them their referral fee.

Make sure your list does not exceed 200 ongoing network referral contacts. Ask yourself what referral source is sending you the most customers and nourish your relationships with them. If you keep it over 200, you are not going to be able to follow everyone on your list, so keep it at 200. However, never stop networking and when you meet someone who is a better referral source than person number 199 on your list, replace them.

Offering people money for referrals is great and productive. However, if people do not know and trust you, they would not refer customers to you, even if you pay a $500 referral fee. Therefore, creating trustful, respectful, and ongoing relationships is the key to successful referral sources.

What is the benefit to the person who gives you referrals? How do they benefit from knowing you? Some people will be happy to just send you new customers. Others will expect to receive a referral back from you to help their business. Others will be excited to attend the dealership's customer appreciation networking events. What is it that your referral source appreciates?

PART I

Chapter 7

THE LAW OF ANXIETY

Both Spider and Honey Bee Car Salespeople want to sell cars and make money. In this chapter, we will tell you what is going on in a customer's mind when they are car shopping so you can sell more cars.

Perception

Most customers expect a Spider Car Salesperson when they think about coming to a dealership. They expect a car salesperson that would try to take advantage of them, try to rob them, and lie to them. This customer's belief is disruptive to the sales process. This belief creates a wall of mistrust and disbelief between a customer and a salesperson that is hard to overcome but necessary to defeat for the business transaction.

There was a time when people thought it was impossible to put passengers in a metal tube and send it to the other side of the globe by air. Thanks to the Wright brothers and other engineers who introduced new ideas, now we call it plane flight. It is difficult to make a change in our perception and ideas about beliefs. However, it is possible. We just have to introduce a new idea.

The problem is that most people do not hold pleasant associations with car dealerships, the sales process, and/or car salespeople. This belief is too large to overcome in a short period of time. However, there are ways to improve customers' perception of car salespeople and dealerships. For example, some dealerships give charitable donations, hold customer appreciation dinners, community events, and other positive community activities that change negative beliefs about car dealerships into positive beliefs.

In summer of 2014, for example, The Equality Club, Inc. hosted an event at a Toyota dealership in Fort Lauderdale to promote diversity, support, and collaboration with the local lesbian, gay, bisexual, transgender, and questioning (LGBTQ) community. This community is an active and fairly affluent group of people with strong and active communications with each other. Sales staff received diversity training prior to the event. Fun activities, great food, prizes, and special promotions for new vehicles that day led to new sales, an improved organizational social image for diversity, and a new stream of committed customers.

Changing customers' perceptions about car dealerships, the sales process, and salespeople is only one step toward creating better relationships with our customers. There are many other factors that influence customers' behavior and the sales process. Most of those are out of the salesperson's control. However, all those customers' emotions can be summarized in a single phenomenon called anxiety.

> "CAR BUYERS' EMOTIONS CAN BE SUMMARIZED IN A SINGLE PHENOMENON CALLED ANXIETY."

Anxiety is a natural reaction to stress. Many customers experience a variety of unpleasant feelings toward the car buying experience. Some customers feel stress when they talk to strangers, have to negotiate, make a significant financial purchase, and/or other reasons, especially if they have unpleasant associations with those steps. Even if a customer's level of stress is very small, it can still lead to anxiety.

Most car buyers experience a very mild level of stress. A customer could feel stress trying to locate your dealership. They had to find the address and transportation to your facility. Customers may also be unfamiliar with the car dealership's area. Even finding the location of the restroom can become a task. Another stressor is overcoming social anxiety about strangers when coming to the dealership. If customers do not know anyone at the dealership, this creates a new social context for them.

Stress ⟶ Anxiety

There are many benefits to anxiety. When we are anxious we are more alert, our memory ability increases, and our heart rate changes. This helps us to respond faster. The level of each customer's anxiety is different but they are usually walking into a dealership anxious.

There are many side effects to anxiety as well. When we get extremely anxious, we may feel physical side effects, like light headed and/or dizzy. It becomes harder to breathe. We may start sweating, blushing, or feeling weak or hyper. Some of us experience an urge to run. Others urge to urinate. There are many more physical side effects of feeling anxious. However, the side effect that we care about the most is a lack of cognitive ability.

Lower Comprehension

*"When anxiety is low,
people are less reactive and more thoughtful…
When anxiety is high,
people can become more reactive and less thoughtful;
system functioning is prone to decline"*
Michael E. Kerr and Murray Bowen

When we are anxious, our ability to comprehend or be logical goes down. The more anxious we are, the less we think. The less anxious we are, the more we are able to comprehend.

"HIGH ANXIETY LEVEL
LOWERS COGNITIVE ABILITY."

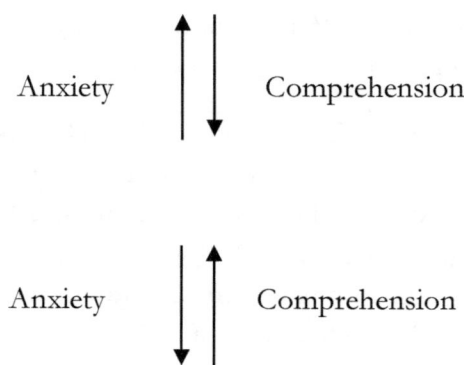

A customer with a master's degree may not understand the simple math of their monthly car payment. No matter how many times and how many ways you break down the numbers for them, they still seem to be confused about the math. Another customer will ask you the same question for the fourth time. Those customers could do this to play dumb. However, the most common reason for this behavior is an increase in customers' anxiety level that lowers their comprehension level.

Customers would like to lower their anxiety. They understand that anxiety is standing in their way of feeling relaxed, comfortable, and enjoying their car purchase. It does not feel good to be anxious for too long. Customers take a variety of actions to lower their anxiety. Here are some examples:

- Customers bringing a friend to a dealership. Most often, customers do not bring their friends to shop at a grocery store with them. They are familiar with the grocery store, the purchasing process, and the products. However, it is different when they shop for a car. Most customers do not bring a friend into a dealership for the friend to advise them on a financial decision or a color of the vehicle. Most of them bring a friend because having a friend next to them lowers their anxiety.

- Customers coming back to the same car salesperson. Customers come back to the same car salesperson, even if they do not like this car salesperson, because he or she is more familiar to them. Being familiar and knowing what to expect could lower customers' levels of anxiety.

- Customers searching the internet and shopping around. They do not shop around and spend days online because they want to. They do it because it is anxiety provoking to go somewhere and not know what to expect, so they are trying to educate themselves.

There are also situations when anxiety is taking control over a customer. In those situations, some customers walk away from the dealership to lower their anxiety. Here are some examples:

- Customers leave the dealership even after they got the best deal. Their anxiety is stronger than their logic. You may show them the numbers and explain the math multiple times but they are not able to comprehend. They are in a state of stress and disbelief.

- Customers walk away from a car even after the paperwork is signed. It can be anxiety provoking to drive a new car. Some customers are afraid of change. For them, even doing something nice for themselves is scary.

General Causes of Anxiety

There are many reasons for an anxiety level to go up. The most common are:

"What if…"

Many of us think about a negative change that could happen in the future, telling ourselves that the worst will happen. Not an action, but just a negative thought of "What if…" is anxiety provoking. What if I lose my job and will not be able to afford this payment? What if this car starts breaking down tomorrow? What if…?

There is no stronger enemy than "What if…" No matter how hard a car salesman tries to overcome the objection, "What if…" will always come up with a new one. The best way to fight "What if…" is by creating trustful relationships where the buyer believes that with any "What if…" they can come back to a salesperson or dealership to work it out.

Help this customer trust the dealership and yourself. Invite the finance manager to assure them about total coverage and maintenance packages. Tell them about your stability as a business. Tell them that they can easily contact you any time after the sale. Tell them that when it is time to trade in the car, you will be here waiting for them.

"ANY NEGATIVE THOUGHT OF
"WHAT IF…"
IS ANXIETY PROVOKING."

Not Knowing

By definition, you know more about the car, the dealership, and the sales process than your customers. Not knowing is a very anxious state. The most anxious part for customers is that they do not know what they do not know. Customers may shop online and ask friends about the car for months before coming to the dealership to increase their knowledge about the vehicle. However, only you can increase their knowledge about you and the dealership.

These customers want to make sure that you are a trusted leader who will take care of their needs. "Sell yourself, sell the dealerships" to this customer before selling them a car. This customer will appreciate stories and verbal direction of the sales process. This will help them know you and the dealership, create common ground, and eventually trust you enough to buy a car. This customer will not buy a car if they do not trust you.

This is also a customer whose anxiety level will go up if you leave them for 15 minutes, for example, to appraise their trade in without informing them what you are doing. They want to know what is going on. Reassure them that everything is ok in every step of the process.

> "ONLY YOU CAN INCREASE YOUR CUSTOMER'S KNOWLEDGE ABOUT YOU AND THE DEALERSHIP."

Change

Most people are more comfortable doing something over and over again than trying to create changes in their life. Why? Because change is anxiety provoking! It is like buying a new house: you know it will have more space and the price is right but you do not want to go through the changes. Moving to a new house, a better house, will require a moving process, meeting new neighbors, and accommodation to different schools for children. Buying a new car, just like a house, is a huge change for some people. The majority of people buy a new car because they have to, not because they want to.

These customers will bring in their 10 year old trade. They will wait to walk into a dealership until their current vehicle breaks down. They will stay faithful to one car brand. They also may not appreciate new technologies, even the ones that make driving an easier and safer experience. This customer would prefer their new car be as similar as possible to their trade in.

Make sure you sit in this customer's car before showing them your product. You may do it as soon as they pull into the dealership or you may ask a buyer to show you their trade-in before you take it to an appraiser. Ask them what they like about their current car. What features would they like to keep or change in their new car? Is anyone else driving this car, for example children, and what do they think are important car features? Let the customer talk. They will tell you what they need and how they will buy.

> "A CUSTOMER WHO DOES NOT LIKE CHANGE WOULD PREFER THEIR NEW CAR TO BE AS SIMILAR AS POSSIBLE TO THEIR TRADE IN."

Tell this customer about benefits of leasing unless they have their mind set on purchasing. With leasing they will always drive a new car, their monthly payment will be lower, and most companies will include a full maintenance package. If you are Honey Bee Salesperson and think "outside the box," after 2-4 years, you can deliver their next car and paperwork to their house. Explain to them that leasing is not about changing your car every 2-4 years, it is about staying in a new car for as long as they like.

When reasons for anxiety are not handled, a person's anxiety level will continue to increase. The next level of feeling anxious is feeling fearful or threatened.

Threat and Self-Protection

When we are anxious, we continue to look for comfort to soothe ourselves. The comfort could be found in familiarity, control, or human connections. However, if comfort is not found, we stop feeling safe. Instead, we feel fear and threat.

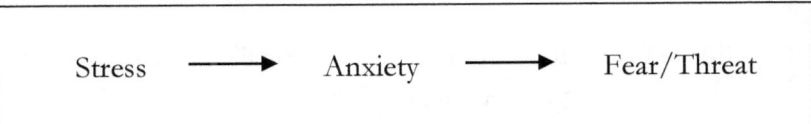

The level of our fear or threat depends on our level of anxiety. The stronger our anxiety level, the stronger our need to self-protect. When our anxiety level is low, we are able to relax, tell a joke, and make thoughtful decisions. When our anxiety level is high, we feel unsafe. When we feel unsafe, we continue to seek self-protection. If comfort is not found, anxiety continues to increase, and people become more expressive in their need to find comfort and self-protect.

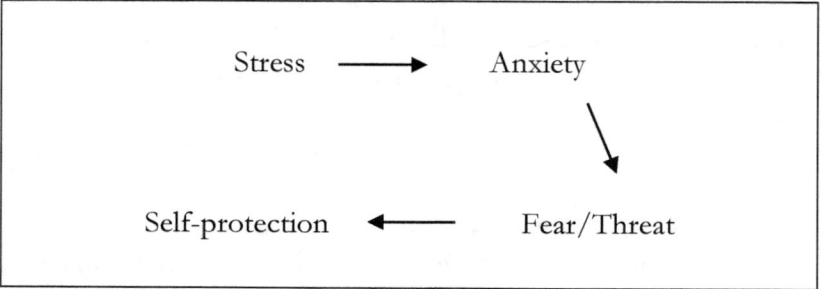

Individuals act differently when they feel threatened. They may utilize different self-protective behaviors. The self-protective behaviors listed below are a customer's reactions to feeling unsafe throughout the car buying process.

- Fight. This customer may challenge everything that you are telling them about the car, price, or process. When this customer is rude to you, it is their way to protect themselves.

- Hide. This customer does not want to talk to anyone. They are often shopping online, or if they come to the dealership, they use phrases like, "I'm just looking."

- Run. This customer runs away from the car salesperson and will walk away from the deal because, for them, it is like talking to their least favorite relative. They can't wait to get away.

- Freeze. They cannot make a decision. They feel overwhelmed with the process so they just stop doing anything about it. It is like shopping for life insurance. Just the thought of your own death is so unpleasant that you never get around to buy it.

- Blame. They will start blaming their third cousin for their credit score, mother for the way they drive, and you for them not being able to afford the car they want.

- Lie. When the customer is lying to you, it is their way to protect themselves.

> "A CUSTOMER WHO FIGHTS, HIDES, RUNS, FREEZES, BLAMES, AND/OR LIES IS JUST TRYING TO PROTECT THEMSELVES AND LOWER THEIR OWN ANXIETY."

All those reactions are natural. Individuals adopt different self-protective techniques throughout their life. But they are not bound to the same self-protective behaviors their entire lives. Their behavior could change depending on a context and level of anxiety. Understanding those processes helps salespeople better understand clients and sell more cars.

Unresolved Conflict

When our methods of self-protection are not able to lower our anxiety level, we continue to stay in the emotional state of threat and fear. In this case, our anxiety level continues to increase. High levels of anxiety can lead to serious conflicts. Deescalating the conflict and lowering an anxiety level needs to be a priority.

Before conflict reaches an uncontrollable state, some customers are able to ask for help by expressing their needs and concerns, but others do not. When conflicts are unresolved, they lead to an increased level of stress, creating a circular pattern where anxiety levels continue to increase.

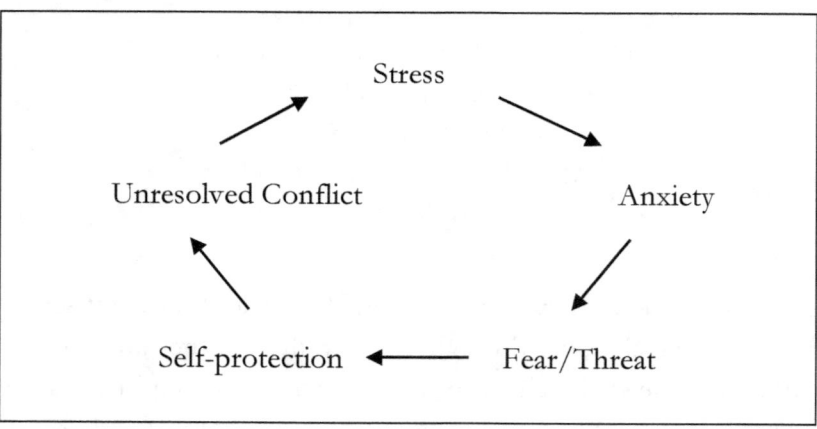

Like a snowball effect, this pattern can become a vicious cycle. If no one tries to bring the anxiety level down by changing the pattern, the conflict can reach an uncontrollable state very quickly.

In order to stop this escalation, an individual must be able to mentally "step outside" of the interaction. Doing that will help you see the pattern you are involved in and separate yourself emotionally from the conflict. When we are able to understand the Law of Anxiety, we are able to understand the cycles we are in and how to manage those cycles.

Unfortunately, many people become involved in those vicious cycles so easily and passionately that it becomes part of them. The more people who get involved in a conflict, the harder it is to escape the cycle of conflict. People become part of the conflict and conflict becomes part of them when they do not know how to separate themselves from the conflict. This cycle is obvious in some car-shopping couples. Those couples participate in the unresolved conflict cycle for so long that it became their natural way of communicating. They may fight over the color of the car like their life depends on it. Those couples will leave the dealership arguing while the salesperson wonders what went wrong.

The problem is that sometimes the cycles of conflict interaction belong to the customers, sometimes to the salespeople, and are sometimes shared among everyone. Those conflicts are so strong because it is hard to take ourselves out of them. We take things personally and become passionate about winning the argument without realizing we are only adding fuel to the fire.

> "TO STOP A CONFLICT, AN INDIVIDUAL MUST BE ABLE TO MENTALLY 'STEP OUTSIDE' OF THE CONFLICT INTERACTION THEY ARE IN."

Creating a Change

The goal of the car salespeople and sales managers is to help clients decrease their level of anxiety. When customers' anxiety levels are lowered, they are relaxed, happy, feel welcome and safe, and they are better able to communicate with you in a friendly, trustful, and beneficial manner. Lowering customers' anxiety increases their ability to think, make decisions, and purchase cars. Increased ability in decision making, in turn, increases buyers' confidence and lowers their anxiety even more.

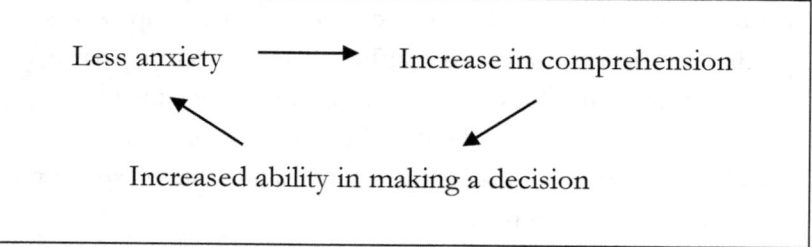

"LOWERING CUSTOMERS' ANXIETY INCREASES THEIR ABILITY TO THINK, MAKE DECISIONS, AND PURCHASE CARS."

In this process, do not try to lower customers' anxiety by yourself. There is a team of professionals on a car showroom floor. Utilize them. You should not be suffering through dealing with high anxiety level customers by yourself. If a customer starts yelling at you about having to wait 15 minutes for a car appraisal, you may easily start feeling your own anxiety level is going up. Protect your own anxiety level. Invite a manager or other professional on the showroom floor into the conversation. They are part of the sales process too.

In a process of lowering customers' anxiety, do not expect to bring customers' anxiety all the way down right away. In fact, some customers will still leave your dealership anxious no matter how hard you try. It is like trying to clean your closet, garage, or an office desk that has so much stuff that you do not know where to start. You are not going to clean it up right away. You will work box by box, tool by tool, document by document. The same concept applies here. Take your time with a customer. Move step by step.

Here are a few steps that could be useful in lowering customer's anxiety:

1. Introduce yourself, the dealership, and managers. Unfamiliarity is scary and anxiety provoking. Tell them about the dealership. Tell them about how the sales process works. Show them the dealership, including the service area, like you would your own house when you have guests. This will help them feel welcome.

2. Trust your intuition and ask questions. Every customer is different so it is hard to predict what their needs are. Be the leader. Guide your customer through the sales process. At the same time, hear your customer and let them tell you what they want. This will tell them that you care. That they can relax and follow your leadership.

3. Ask them what they would like to accomplish. They will tell you how to sell them a car.

4. Do not try to lower customers' anxiety by yourself. When necessary, ask your manager to talk to your customer and reassure them about the process or answer their questions.

5. Make their family, friend, or other guest that is influencing their decision your friend. The friend's anxiety could be transferred onto your customer. The friend's confidence in a purchase could also influence the customer. Try to answer the friend's questions and concerns to bring their anxiety down as well.

6. Make them laugh. Laughter strengthens relationships, attracts others to us, enhances teamwork, helps defuse conflict, and promotes group bonding. Producing a familiar "ha, ha, ha," triggers an increase in endorphins, the brain chemicals known for their feel-good effect. This helps everyone feel relaxed, safe, and joyful. Laughter has many positive links with mental health. For instance, laughter dissolves distressing emotions, helps us relax and recharge, reduces stress, and increases energy. If you do not have good jokes, borrow from your coworkers.

7. Educate customers but at the same time do not buy back your sale. Do not educate them about everything. You do not want to make your customer feel overwhelmed. If they start yawning, it's a sign that they are too tired to hear this information. Simply answer these customers' questions. Some customers care about safety, others about speed. Appeal to their hot buttons.

8. Tell stories. Listening to stories will help customers shift their focus from the things that make them anxious to

more entertaining things. Keep your stories short, diversity inclusive, and relevant to the topic of discussion.

9. Stay relaxed and confident. Your confidence is contagious. If you are not confident in your product, do not expect for your customer to be confident.

Chapter 8

#1 CAR SALESPERSON'S MISTAKE

Salespeople get anxious too. We feel more anxious about some parts of the sale process than the other. Some of us feel more anxious when we are doing a "walk around" of the vehicle, others when we are negotiating. We could get anxious even after selling cars for many years. Sometimes anxiety feels like a positive flow of energy, for example, when we complete the sale and get adrenaline in our veins. Unfortunately, most often it feels less exciting. We could feel nervous when we are in need of funds. We could feel aggressive when other salespeople "skate" us. Sometimes our anxiety could be directly connected to the fear of speaking, rejection, presenting, performing, and many other worries.

As we hope you realize by now, being anxious is not necessarily a bad thing. Anxiety helps us stay safe. Thanks to anxiety, we stay alert when we drive. It is negative when your level of anxiety is too high that we are not able to function productively. It is even worse when your anxiety level is higher than your customers'.

A salesperson's high anxiety level can lead to a similar negative cycle of conflict that we discussed earlier. This cycle could be easily observed in a salesperson influenced by a very common reason for anxiety – fear of failure.

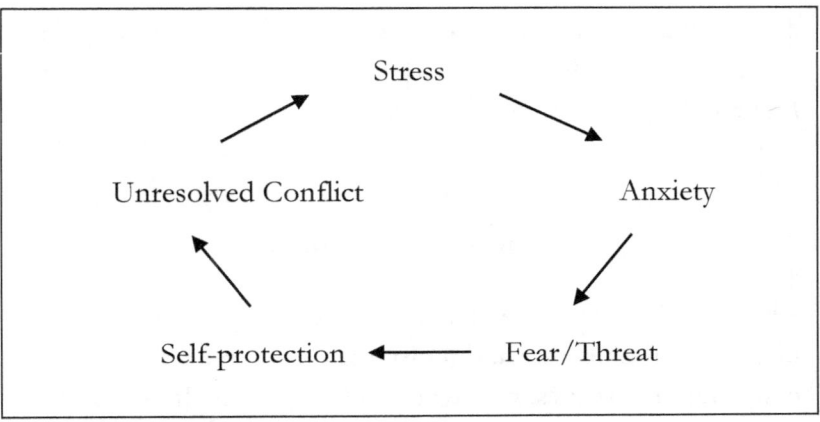

The cycle could start with this salesperson feeling stress because he or she did not sell a car for a week. The salesperson's fear of not performing could continue to increase with each passing day without a sale. This high anxiety level will start to influence multiple aspects of the salesperson's life and personality. For example, he or she could become more sensitive to rejections by the customers. The secret to selling a car is to listen your customer and stay logical, which is almost impossible when you are anxious. The anxious salesperson will not be able to overcome a customer's objections to sell a car.

The bigger problem caused by a fear or failure is not losing a sale but creating a conflict with a customer who would then make sure their friends and family would not buy a car from that salesperson and the dealership. This could happen way too easily when a salesperson is motivated by anxiety and fear of failure rather than calmness and logic. This leads to even fewer sales for this salesperson, higher stress, and increased fear of failure.

Do not make anxiety your enemy. Make it your friend. Embrace your fears and walk hand-to-hand with your anxiety.

Try to understand where your anxiety came from and why that could be important to you. Understanding your anxiety is the first and biggest step to conquering it.

Anxiety is Contagious

Anxious salespeople run all over the dealership. They do not know the sales process and jump from one topic to the next, confusing themselves, managers, and customers. It does not matter what they or you are anxious about. What does matter is that anxiety is contagious. Anxiety is like the flu, moving from a family member to a coworker, to a stranger at the grocery store. When you are anxious, everyone around you becomes anxious.

> "WHEN YOU ARE ANXIOUS, EVERYONE AROUND YOU BECOMES ANXIOUS."

Anxiety is transferable. The same way you can feel when your customer is anxious, your customer can feel that you are anxious. Customers may interpret your anxiety in different ways. They may think you are anxious because you are lying or because you are selling a bad product. When you are new in a car business, you will be more anxious than most experienced car salespeople. Tell your customer if you are new. This way they could read your anxiety as a learning process.

Threat and Self-protection

Just like our customers, we are engaging in self-protective behavior stimulated by our anxiety.

- Fight. We argue with our colleagues, managers, service writers, and customers.
- Hide. We hide from sales managers, colleagues, and even customers, especially if there is something wrong and we do not know how to fix it.
- Run. We run away from our problems.
- Freeze. When we feel overwhelmed, we stop selling cars, making phone calls, or talking to people.
- Blame. We blame our lack of success on family members, managers, or product. Everyone and everything, but not ourselves.
- Lie. We lie to a customer when we are threatened with losing a sale. The truth is you are not going to get sale by lying to a customer. If you do not believe in a process and product you sell, you will never sell it.

The positive news is that calmness is also transferable. If you are able to be calm and confident in a sales process, the client becomes calm and confident in the process as well. There is no simple answer to how we can stay calm and lower our anxiety. We are all different. For each of us, the answer is different.

Some of us may find it helpful to talk to a manger, mentor, friend, family member, colleague, or other professional. For others, it is a question of product and process knowledge. Knowledge and understanding lowers our anxiety. It is also ethical to know what you are selling. Memorize the sale process and try to follow the same path every single sale. Remember, people follow those who know where they are going.

When you have a high anxiety level, remembering at least one way to deal with stress could be difficult. List your own 5 ways of dealing with stress and anxiety now, to make it easier for later. Some of you would find a certain type of music more soothing, while others find comfort in exercising. Please try to avoid substances abuse and other behaviors that may harm you and others around you, no matter how relaxing it may feel at the time.

Your ways of dealing with stress and anxiety:

Chapter 9

THE LAW OF CALMNESS

"For every action, there is an equal and opposite reaction."
Newton's Third Law

A salesperson is affected by a client's anxiety the same way the client is affected by the salesperson's anxiety. In the same way, a salesperson is affected by a client's calmness the way the client is affected by the salesperson's calmness.

The Law of Calmness states that by keeping ourselves calm, and understanding our reactions due to the anxiety, we are able to view a situation from a place of genuine care and understanding. From here, we can see and honor multiple realities, and build relationships based on trust. Calmness helps us to reach mutually beneficial relationships and sell more cars.

Have you noticed that the less you stress about money or sales, the more you sell? It seems that when business is bad, everything is bad, and when it is good, everything gets better. You may have a rough week but as soon as you sell a car, everything becomes brighter. That rude customer from this morning just seems to be forgotten, lunch tastes more delicious, and the next sale seems to come more easily.

That is The Law of Calmness at work. When we are not stressed about the sale, we radiate confidence, comfort, and stability. We become satisfied with whatever we are doing and we enjoy the process more than the outcome. Buyers can sense that energy. They cannot explain it but they are drawn to it.

When customers feel your confidence, comfort, and stability, they seem to not want to leave you. For them, it is a pleasure to spend time with you. They see you as a friend they can trust and will work with you productively. They come back to bring you gifts, invite you for lunch, and most importantly, send you referrals.

> Calmness ⟶ Confidence, Comfort, & Stability

When there is an emergency, we call 911. We trust people in uniform to take care of the situation and our anxiety. Their presence is a sign of hope that community needs will be met. We prefer to follow their guidance. A calm car salesperson is like that professional in a uniform. They can assess the situation and take control over the car buying process. They are leaders, not persuaders.

> "CALMNESS RADIATES CONFIDENCE, COMFORT, AND STABILITY."

Listening

Listening is the best way for a salesperson to let the buyer know that you are a leader and not a persuader. Listening is the most powerful form of influence. Salespeople that master listening techniques do not sit quietly but ask questions and acknowledge what the customer is saying. Some customers will not tell you anything until you ask. In addition, it lets the buyer know that the salesperson cares.

> "LISTENING IS THE MOST POWERFUL FORM OF INFLUENCE."

When salespeople talk, they operate from their own assumptions. Their actions are driven by guess, trial, and error. This can become time consuming, anxiety provoking, and lead to loss of time and sales. When salespeople are listening, they operate from clues that customers give to them.

People are best convinced by reasons they themselves discover. A customer will tell the salesperson how to sell them a car if only the salesperson asks. The most common questions are:

- What brought you in today?

This question allows a customer to express their goals for seeing you.

- What features do you like most in your current car?

Even if you think a customers' car is junk, it might be a treasure to them. They drove it longer than you did and learned to appreciate its benefits. Customer will give you the most interesting clues on what they like or dislike about cars when you ask them about their current car. Some customers appreciate cruise control and safety features, while others fall in love with their change holder.

Ask a customer for details about those benefits or negatives they can name. For example, if a customer brings up gas mileage efficiency, ask them how often they visit the gas station. Do they pay for the gas themselves or get reimbursed? Any information will help you know your customer better and tell you how to sell them a car.

Those questions also allow the customer to feel like an expert. Even customers who would never discuss cars voluntarily could easily talk about a personal driving experience. Feeling like an expert will help customers gain control over their anxiety and help them feel comfortable. Like a house, the customer's car is a part of their comfort zone. Talking about the customer's car will help lower his or her anxiety by bringing them back to their comfort zone.

> "A CUSTOMER WILL TELL YOU
> HOW TO SELL THEM A CAR."

- What interested you most in (the car they named)?

It is exciting and easier when a customer tells you exactly what car they want. However, do you know why they want that vehicle? Are they looking for space, features, or want to impress their neighbors? Knowing what the customer likes the most in a vehicle they choose could give you strong clue about how to close them.

- What is your biggest concern in the car buying process?

Is the customer's concern about maintenance, insurance, comfort, or maybe price? You would not know until you ask. However, by asking customer this question up front, you introduce a safe space to discuss their concerns without guessing. This will help you overcome most challenges. It also will let the customer know that you are concerned and care about them, giving you extra points.

- Do not ask "How may I *help* you?" ask "How may I serve you?"

"How may I help you?" assumes your significance over the customer. Most customers would prefer to feel significant, which could lead them to answer, "I do not need help."

How you ask is more important than what you ask. Calmness radiates confidence and importance in every question you ask. At the same time, when you are anxious, sometimes even you do not know why you are asking that same question.

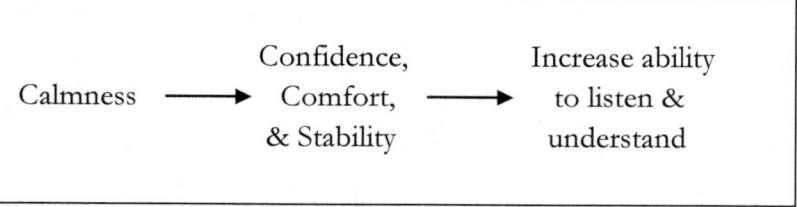

Remaining calm is often hard. Is it even harder to sell a car when you are anxious. Do you remember earlier when we talked about how, when our anxiety level goes up, our ability to think clearly (comprehension) goes down? At that point we are in reaction, not response mode. In the same way, when we are less anxious (more calm), we are able to assess the situation more clearly and use it to our advantage.

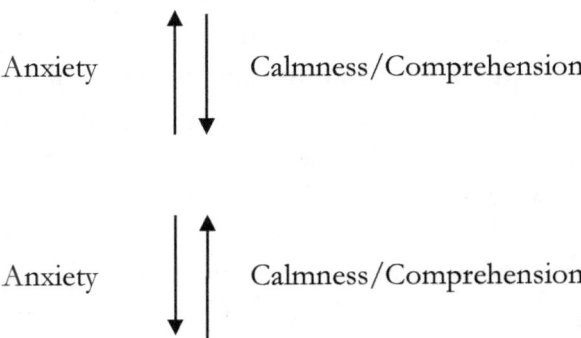

Shaheed was working with an older lady who used a walker to move carefully around the dealership. Do not let her appearance confuse you. She was an ex-detective from New York, had a strong handshake, and confident tone of voice. She shared that she always had structure in her life and wanted to continue following it. Unfortunately, this structure did not prevent her from having a low credit score. She could not afford a payment higher than $420 a month but her credit score increased her interest rate and would not allow her to get the car for lower than $500 a month, no matter how long her term or how cheap the car. After long hours of working the car business magic, nothing seemed to work. Thankfully, right before the last option seemed to fail, Shaheed was able to think outside the box and put the deal together.

There is a loyalty program for Toyota customers on a new car. The program offers a low interest rate for customers who pay their car payment on time for 12 months straight. With this program in mind, the deal was put together. The lady would still pay $500 a month, but for the next 12 months she would get an $80 check from the dealership to help her reach her $420 a month payment. The deal was that, after paying her

12th payment, she would come back and get new car, with a lower interest rate, for the same $420 a month payment or even lower. Everyone wins. The lady was a happy car owner, Shaheed made a sale and guaranteed repeat business 12 months after the sale, and the dealership will continue to utilize this new creative tool and attract a positive reputation.

The monthly payment was most important to this customer. She did not care how long her term was or what car she drove. This story is a great example of building rapport, asking questions, and remaining calm enough to think outside the box.

Acknowledgment and Response

There would be no point for a salesperson to ask a buyer a question if he or she completely ignores the customer's response and does not utilize the customer's answer to sell them a car. There are two key communication steps to any answer or comment that your customer makes: acknowledgment and response.

Acknowledgment

Acknowledgment is a way to let the speaker know that you are listening and follow what they are saying. Acknowledgment is the first step to successful communication and relationship building. The most common ways for the listener to let the speaker know that he or she is listening is by cues, such as responding with hand gestures and eye contact, facial movement, brief vocalizations and grunts, and many more. This is everything from sitting in a mirroring posture to your customer, looking them in the eye, nodding your head, and responding with "Aha," "Mmhm," "Really?" "Wow," "No kidding," "Ok," and many more.

Unfortunately, a lot of couples experience difficulty in that step. A wife may say, "My husband (partner) does not listen to me." She could become very stressed, which could lead to a serious argument in the relationship. While the wife may be right and her husband (partner) wishes to mute her like a T.V., most likely her husband (partner) does listen to her but does not acknowledge it. Dr. John Gottman, a researcher of couples' relationships, in his book *The Marriage Clinic* (1999) called it stonewalling. Dr. Gottman stated that stonewalling is one of the highest cues in a couple's relationships that predicts divorce.

In a sale process, a salesperson that practices stonewalling would look away from a customer for a long time when the customer is talking to him or her. That salesperson's body would appear "frozen." They would not move their head, hands, or even an eyebrow. They would vocalize hardly at all. This could be the salesperson's way to show respect to a customer, or the salesperson may be shocked that he or she actually got a customer to talk to them. However the customer would view this behavior as ignorance.

A customer who works with a salesperson who does not acknowledge them with any facial or vocal responses feels like a person in front of a frozen computer screen. When a cursor on a computer screen does not respond to our commands from a mouse or keyboard, for some of us, we become mad at the technology.

Do not be a frozen computer screen. Use basic verbal and non-verbal cues to let your customer know you are listening to them. At the same time, do not become a creep about it. Do not engage in a staring contest. Look around once in a while. Successful communication and relationship building is a balance.

> "ACKNOWLEDGMENT IS A WAY TO LET THE SPEAKER KNOW YOU ARE LISTENING AND FOLLOWING WHAT THEY ARE SAYING."

In the Corporation Clinic's workshops and coaching sessions, we go over a few tips on customer acknowledgment. One of those tips is called echoing.

Echoing

Echoing is repeating what the customer said, giving it back to them. This will assure the customer that you are listening to him or her, show them that you care, and that you understood them the way they want to be understood. This is also a great way to stop the customer from talking without interruption and getting to business without being rude.

Echoing is a technique. Do not simply repeat everything the customer says. Repeat only what is important and in a respectful manner. Two magic phrases will assure that you acknowledge your customer by using echoing. Those phrases are "So what you are telling me is…" and "Correct me if I am wrong. Are you saying that…" For example, the customers keep telling you about their daughter's soccer practice and how they have to pick up her friends for carpooling. You may respond, "So what you are telling me is, that your daughter enjoys soccer and that you would prefer a car that would comfortably fit all her friends for carpooling?"

Another example is a customer who complains to you about their previous car salesperson, who took advantage of them. You may respond, "Correct me if I am wrong. Are you saying that your last experience with a car buying process was not pleasant and this time you would like to make sure you will work with a salesperson that understands your needs and respects your budget?"

Response

The response step is self explanatory. When the customer tells you, "I want a white truck," show them the white truck. When the customer tells you, "My partner must have heated seats," make sure to add the heated seats feature to the car or find a car that includes that feature.

When your anxiety is too high, you may experience difficulty in this step. This usually appears like memory loss. For example, your manager told you to bring them a stock number of the car but you come back to the manager with the customer's driver's license. There is a high possibility that you did not do it to get on the manager's nerves. Most likely, some customer or finance manager will get you off track and you totally forgot that the manager asked for the stock number of the car. In those situations, try to breathe, slow down, and write things down.

Chapter 10

THE CALM-DRIVEN SALE

Calm-Driven Selling is a sales process that builds on relationships of support and trust for the purpose of receiving information and lowering everyone's anxiety. The sale comes from collaborative, mutually beneficial relationships.

Customers buy from people they like, trust, and feel comfortable with. That is the heart and soul of the sales process. Shared values and mutual understanding creates positive relationships and increases trust. Avoid anything that can damage the trust the customer has in you.

> "CUSTOMERS BUY FROM
> PEOPLE THEY LIKE, TRUST, AND
> FEEL COMFORTABLE WITH."

We know about anxiety that:

- Customers walk into the dealership anxious. They have different levels of anxiety.
- The higher a customer's anxiety, the less rational they are.
- The higher the salesperson's anxiety, the harder it is to concentrate on what the customer is saying.

- Anxiety creates chaos and decreases sales transactions.

We know about calmness that:

- When customers feel calm, they feel welcome and able to negotiate rationally.
- When the salesperson feels calm, they are able to use the client's language to sell a car.
- Calm-Driven sales lead to positive relationship building and win-win sales transactions.

Calm-Driven Selling is about controlling your own anxiety as a sales person and helping clients to lower theirs. Because calmness is contagious, your level of calmness is more significant than your customers'.

Katia once worked with a family that was looking for their daughter's first car. The daughter knew exactly what she wanted and the father knew exactly how much he was willing to spend. This was a pretty typical situation except this family strongly insisted on staying away from the showroom without a particular reason.

When the family was asked again to come inside the showroom after the test drive, the energy in the family drastically shifted. They liked a car and wanted to negotiate while staying outside. A flexible and professional manager came outside to meet the family, talked about the car, and invited them inside one more time. The more the family was asked to come inside, the more anxious the father would get and, with him, the rest of the family. An anxiety transferred from the father to the rest of the family because anxiety is contagious.

Family members are especially attuned to each other. If one family member gets anxious, the whole family will transmit this information faster than a stranger like a salesperson would. In this situation, the shift in anxiety level was so drastic that even the salesperson was able to feel the difference.

When the family finally walked into the showroom, the father started to move his hands very fast and speak louder. These actions were motivated by the increase in anxiety level. After the first pencil was presented, the family quickly stood up and walked out of the showroom. The manager decided to let the family leave.

As soon as the family was outside of the showroom, the fast hand movements slowed down, voice tones lowered, and the family wanted to continue talking. Outside was a comfort zone for this family. Outside, they felt safe and their anxiety was not in the way of their logic. Katia invited the family to look at the car again and the conversation continued. The family wanted to take their time and go home. She respected their choice and followed up with phone calls. Keeping customers in their comfort zone created a respectful and collaborative space for the business transaction and building a healthy relationship. After few phone calls, the family came back to the dealership and bought three cars, one for the daughter, one for a niece, and one for a nephew, all in one day.

> "KEEPING CUSTOMERS IN THEIR COMFORT ZONE CREATES A RESPECTFUL AND COLLABORATIVE SPACE FOR BUSINESS TRANSACTIONS AND HEALTHY RELATIONSHIPS."

What made this sales transaction possible was taking a career-building, relationship-driven, and referral-oriented approach instead of a here and now sale. Allowing customers to stay in their zone of comfort kept them calm and allowed Katia to create relationships based on trust, respect, and comfort.

Anxiety As a Salesperson's Ally

The first step to inviting calmness and lowering your anxiety level is to notice how your emotional state is different when you are selling a car, in comparison to when you are talking to your friends. Are you becoming louder or more shy? Does a wave of energy come over you or can you barely move? Are you becoming overly excited or does your emotional state not change at all? Those questions are difficult to answer right away. Most sales-people need to talk to a few customers before they can truly understand their own emotions. Please take your time to answer those questions.

The second step to inviting calmness and lowering your anxiety level is to see benefit in the physical and emotional changes that anxiety brings. What matters is not just the physical and emotional changes anxiety brings, but also how we respond to them. The goal is to view the way stress changes our body and emotions, particularly in the sales process, and learn to see these as positive rather than negative.

> "WHAT MATTERS IS NOT WHAT PHYSICAL AND EMOTIONAL CHANGES ANXIETY BRINGS, BUT HOW WE RESPOND TO THEM."

Anxiety is inevitable. It is up to you to determine if anxiety is your ally or enemy. Sometimes anxiety could be our ally. There are some benefits to short term anxiety:

- It makes you social. When we are anxious, our level of oxytocin, the cuddle hormone, increases. It orients you to things that strengthen close relationships, makes you crave physical contact, enhances your empathy, makes you more willing to help and support, and motivates you to seek support.
- It increases empathy and cooperation.
- Just like adrenalin, it creates changes in your heart rate, which could help in extreme situations where your survival depends on your ability to react fast.

Notice that these reactions to stress focus on building a relationship, support, and collaboration to achieve a safe and comfortable environment.

Anxiety As a Customer's Ally

The same benefits of anxiety apply to customers. Use customers' anxiety to your advantage. The customer who is anxious will look for a human connection. Take your time to build relationships with customers. Talk to them, offer them a coffee, ask them what they would like to accomplish. The goal is to avoid premature walk-around or discussion of numbers. Build a relationship first.

When a client's anxiety grows, positive communication diminishes. If their anxiety level is not deescalated, it leads to an increase in feelings of threat and fear. In cases of threat and fear, we naturally search for self-protection. Conflict increases if protection is not reached, leading to another, stronger, and escalating stress level.

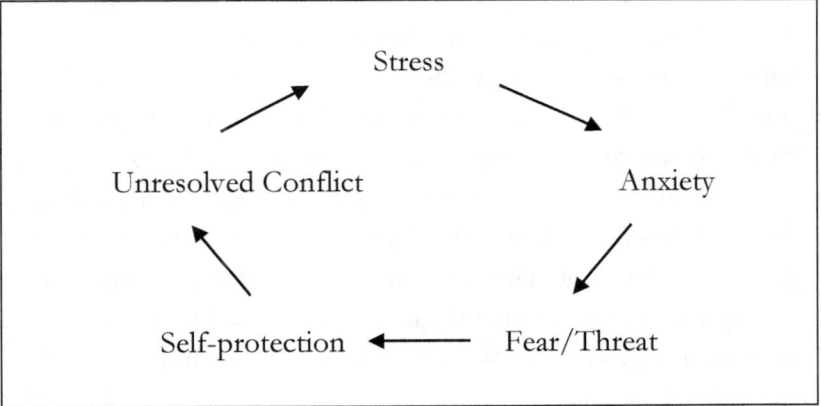

Build a relationship with your customer where he or she knows that you are listening and hear them, that you care about their concerns, and will help them to deescalate their problems.

"BUILD A RELATIONSHIP FIRST."

The biggest goal is to reach a relationship level where customers feel welcomed, respected, and safe to express their concerns. When clients feel safe to tell you about their concerns, you reach their trust. This customer would be happy with the sale process, their new car, their payment, and your service. They would tell their friends, colleagues, and family about the positive buying experience you provided. This can lead to more sale transactions for you.

Common Factors that Influence a Change/Sale

A car salesperson is like a therapist. They meet a client, hear their concerns, create change in a customer's life, and charge money at the end of the session. Car salespeople are unique from other sales professionals. In comparison with a telemarketer or a cashier at the grocery store, car salespeople spend time with their customers. You have an opportunity to create special relationships with your customers. For a salesperson, a sale, like a therapy session is a relational process that aims to create change that helps customers find a solution they are looking for. The difference is that a therapist aims to change customers' relational patterns and a car salesperson aims to change customers' method of transportation.

In 1992, Michael Lambert, in J. C. Norcross & M. R. Goldfried's *Handbook of Psychotherapy Integration*, studied common factors in psychotherapy that stimulate change in families. The similarities between the work of a psychotherapist and a car salesperson allows us to transmit his results into the common factors of influence that stimulate a sale.

Common factors of influence on sale transactions:

> 55% - the customer factor. Influences driving customers' decision to purchase a car most often are outside of the salesperson's control. They are based on customers' factors only.

> 30% - the relationship factor. Relationships between a customer and salesperson have the strongest influence

on customers' decision of a car purchase. The more those relationships are positive, respectful, caring, thoughtful, and considerate, the stronger influence they have on a sales transaction.

15% - the sale technique factor. Know the product and sales process but do not depend only on that.

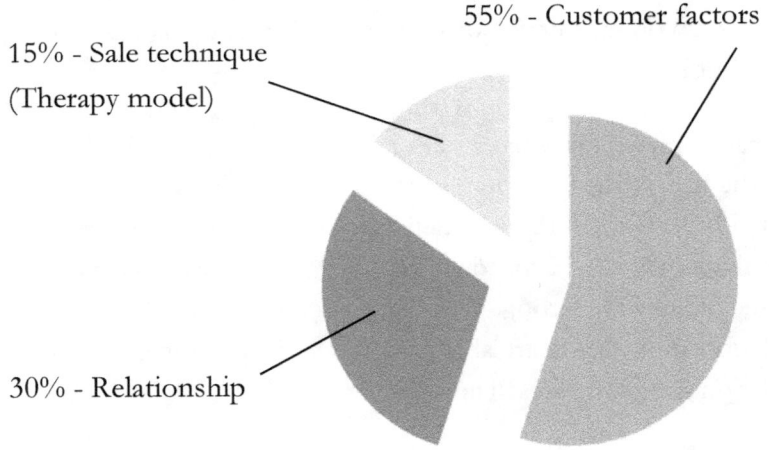

Those findings were revolutionary. Even though those numbers should be considered as general trends rather than an exact percentage, they show the significance of human relationships and communication over techniques, procedures, and tactics that a therapist and salesperson implement to influence change.

Do not disregard the benefits and necessity of product knowledge and sales procedure. A car salesperson is still required to know the difference between Kia Soul and BMW

X5. Based on common factors theory, the success of your sale depends on your product knowledge 15% of the time, which is almost every sixth car, so study safety and comfort features but do not assume people will buy a car from you because you can break a car apart and build it back with your eyes closed.

Also, do not be discouraged that 55% of the time, you have no idea what will influence your customer to buy a car. A customer could be influenced by the location of a dealership, the color of your table, the weather, a job promotion, or divorce. You may never know what really made this customer buy but it is ok.

What is important, what makes a huge difference, is that 30% of the time, the sale depends on nothing but the salesperson's relationships with buyers. Many salespeople and managers think all they need is product knowledge or a magical closing phrase. They are wrong. What they need is an ability to build relationships. If you are able to hold a conversation and build a relationship, you can sell anything.

Large companies like Avon, Mary Kay, or Amway understand the power and success of human communication. That was a secret to their fast growing success and stability. Based on that knowledge, they built a sales structure where each buyer can receive an individual approach and cultivate ongoing relationships with their seller. These business are structured on relationship building.

> "30% OF THE TIME,
> THE SALE DEPENDS ON
> THE SALESPERSON'S RELATIONSHIP
> WITH THE BUYER."

Human Communication

The secret to all relationship building is joining. Verbal and non-verbal communications help salespeople join with their customers. Verbal communication is communication through language. Non-verbal communication is communication through expression, gesture, and posture. Through verbal and non-verbal communication, people express their happiness, worries, celebrations, and concerns. The goal of both verbal and non-verbal communication is to build respectful relationships, where our differences are accepted and honored. Any type of discrimination will ruin respectful relationship building.

Communication ⟶ Respectful Relationship

Through respectful relationships, customers are provided a space where they can voice their concerns about the car buying process and find an opportunity to negotiate solutions to those concerns. The salesperson who takes time to listen and hear their customers, acknowledge what they are communicating, and respect their choices has a higher chance to sell a customer a car and receive referrals.

Remaining calm and not taking things personally will help salespeople create stronger and more respectful communication. This is not an easy task. Customers could be very rude and derogatory. The secret of remaining calm and not taking customer's behavior personally is remembering that most customers are rude because they are anxious, not because something about you is wrong. Not you, but their anxiety makes them fight, hide, run, freeze, blame, and lie.

When a salesperson is able to separate themself from a customer's anxiety, he or she is able to remain calm. The salesperson is then able to express and hear concerns. A salesperson who is calm can communicate in a genuine and caring way. Your customer can feel it. You can feel it. This calmness transfers to the customer, which helps build relationships and completes a business transaction.

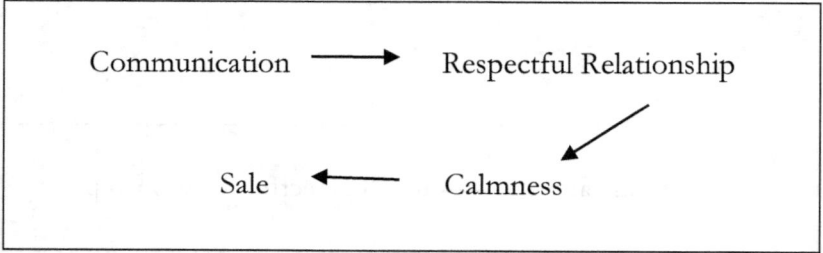

Respectful relationships will build positive emotions. When a customer likes you, they will like a car and a dealership. Their logic will support, rather than drive, the decision to buy a car. When a customer likes you, their mind will justify the decision to buy a car from you with logic and facts.

PART III

Chapter 11

TRADITIONAL VS. CALM-DRIVEN SELLING

Negotiation is the traditional way of looking at a car sale. The salesperson offers a car. In return, the buyer offers money. The goal, in the traditional sale process, a salesperson builds a value of the vehicle to be able to charge more money. The rest is negotiation.

Relationship is the Calm-Driven way of looking at a car sale. For the customer, negotiation is not a priority. Respect, trust, and comfort make a difference for the customer in the sales transaction. Only after relationships are established will the buyer negotiate. The goal of the salesperson is to build a respectful relationship with a buyer to be able to maximize profit. The rest is paperwork.

In a Calm-Driven buying/selling transaction, the customer may read reviews, buy a car online, and receive and give instant worldwide feedback on their buying experience. In the Calm-Driven Selling era of relationship building, dealerships cannot afford to operate from the traditional way of negotiating, which views relationship building as secondary to business success.

In a traditional business transaction based on negotiation, there are winners and losers. Satisfaction from a business transaction equals the amount of money the dealership or customer loses or gains. However, even when a dealership feels that they gave the car away, a customer may still feel that he or she has been taken advantage of. This leads to a negative reviews and surveys.

In a relationship based sales transaction, everyone is a winner. Satisfaction in the business transaction equals the amount of respect and confidence both sides give to each other. Those relationships promote equality and respect. Both sides come out as winners of new beneficial relationships.

People simply will not buy a car from you unless they like and trust you. At any store and in any relationship, we expect to be treated with respect. When someone treats us as badly, we as customers simply walk out, shop at another store, and tell others how bad the first store was. The loss is not on the customer. The situation could be different if this store is the only one around for a long distance or the only one to offer the product we need. We may still buy the product from that store, even when we had a bad relational experience.

Unfortunately for a car salesperson, there is nothing unique about their car or dealership. There are many other dealerships that may offer similar or the same car and services. In this case, the product the car dealership offers is not unique and buyers' decisions will depend on a relationship with a salesperson.

> "NEGOTIATION
> IS THE TRADITIONAL WAY
> OF LOOKING AT A CAR SALE.
>
> RELATIONSHIP
> IS THE CALM-DRIVEN WAY
> OF LOOKING AT A CAR SALE."

A Letter to Colleagues

The traditional era of negotiation, in comparison with the Calm-Driven era of relationship, has also maintained different influences on relationships among colleagues. The traditional negotiation era views relationships of employees and managers in the car industry as an exchange of manpower for money. In this model, relationships on the job are treated as negotiations. The biggest benefit of this business model is that salespeople can make a lot of money. The car business is financially rewarding, which draws many people into the business. The biggest downside of this model is that those relationships are based on competition, survival, and lone man strategies. Team building is almost non-existent.

The Calm-Driven relationships era views relationships of employees and managers in the car industry as an exchange of support, motivation, recognition, education, and respect. In this model, our work relationships with managers, employees, and coworkers are based on money and negotiations. No one can diminish the importance of money. Money is very important in most jobs and the payment structure of the car business has worked well for many years. However, relationships could be better for everyone.

A lone man mentality is damaging. Sales people and managers are in competition for the highest financial performance. The top dogs in the business receive a lot of recognition and benefits, even though they are envied by others. The dogs that do worse do not survive long enough to learn the proper sales procedures and product knowledge. The turnover rate will catch them before they catch themselves. They make many mistakes on possible buyers and leave soon after, making room for the next newbie to try to sell a car by trial and error.

There will always be a competitive environment in the car business and this is a good thing. Competition drives us to action and brings money to the dealership. The competition is not a problem. The problem is a salespersons' relationships with each other. Creating stronger relationships based on respect, understanding, and support will help not only individual salespeople but also the dealership and sales community as a whole.

The car business is fascinating and magnetizing. People who have experienced the benefits of the car business do not want to leave it. For this reason, many salespeople would leave a dealership but not the car business. They would just move to a different dealership. Some salespeople would move for the financial opportunities. However, a majority move to another dealership in search of a more respectful, understanding, and cooperative work environment.

Chapter 12

KEEP YOUR CUSTOMERS CLOSE AND YOUR COWORKERS CLOSER

The majority of car salespeople enjoy the car business. They enjoy presenting, delivering, and talking about cars. They enjoy meeting new car buyers, especially these who pay the most money. However, when it comes to relationships among salespeople, we do not like each other very much. We see each other as competitors. A new salesperson is looked at with concern and rarely welcomed with open arms. An experienced salesperson is looked at with an attitude of scarcity and is suspected of trying to skate others. A top performer salesperson is looked at with envy. A low performer salesperson is questioned about their longevity in the car business.

Better relationships among salespeople could create a stronger support system. Salespeople could teach and improve each other's skills to increase their performance. They could team up on their marketing efforts. However, only a few salespeople will choose that route. Most salespeople wish to avoid mutually beneficial relationships with colleagues because the competitive environment prevents them from wishing success to their opponents, even when an absence of those relationships is more harmful to themselves than to others.

It is up to you what relationships you will create with other salespeople. Many salespeople enjoy a lone work environment where everyone depends on himself or herself. As long as no conflict is created, we can sustain relationships with other salespeople in a respectful and supportive manner. The problem arises when a salesperson has to deal with conflict. In these situations, the salesperson has to deal with a conflict instead of focusing on their career.

If the salesperson chooses to work on resolving a conflict, he or she looses an opportunity to sell a car at that time. If the salesperson chooses to sell a car, he or she looses an opportunity to fix a conflict with a colleague at that time. No matter what a salesperson would choose to do, he or she will experience an opportunity cost.

> *"Opportunity Cost is the loss of potential gain from other alternatives when one alternative is chosen"*
> New Oxford American Dictionary

Conflicts with our coworkers can take our full attention and overshadow other important aspects of our life. It is difficult to concentrate on selling a car in a hostile work environment or while experiencing conflict, change, or loss at home. We must deescalate conflict first. However, if we spend all our time on creating and deescalating conflicts, we will not have time to sell cars.

Some of these conflicts could create positive outcomes. We could learn, negotiate, and create new opportunities in our relationships. Unfortunately, sometimes those conflicts get worse and require more attention, effort, and time—leaving less time and concentration on selling cars and creating productive relationships with customers.

Sometimes conflicts are so strong, they dominate our focus. In these situations, we do not pay attention to the customer's needs, seem not able to close them, or even send customers to work with another salesperson. Instead, we choose to continue arguing to resolve conflicts. No matter how hard we try, this happens too often. This is where the phrase, "Leave your home problems at home and work problems at work" came from. Unfortunately, it is easier said than done.

Conflicts at work, in addition to aggression, disrespect, and long wait hours could lead salespeople to job dissatisfaction. Many salespeople bring work problems home. Their energy is tied to a long day with no sale or arguments with coworkers. When this negative energy is brought home, it creates stress and discomfort with the family.

Work problems ⟶ Family problems

Stress and conflict at home with family could easily escalate and be carried by the salesperson to work.

Family problems ⟶ Work problems

It does not matter if conflict or stress started from home and is carried to work, or started at work and is carried home. What matters is that they could easily influence each other and continue to escalate. This process creates a negative cycle that is hard to interrupt.

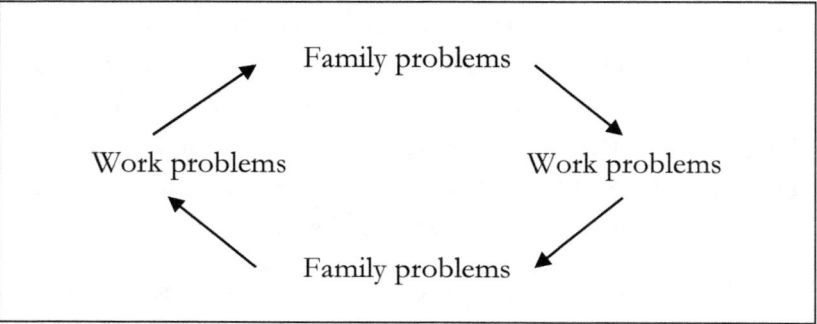

Creating a respectful, supportive, and caring work environment where conflicts could be easily discussed and deescalated will allow you to avoid opportunity cost, concentrate on selling cars, and have fewer conflicts at home. This is easier said than done. Perhaps we could start by creating friendlier work and home environments while keeping ourselves aware of the consequences that our actions could bring for better understanding of self and others.

Bring on the Calm

In case of an emergency situation in an airplane, the oxygen mask will come out. In those situations, you are asked to remain calm and put an oxygen mask on yourself before assisting others. The fact is simple; you cannot assist others if you need more help than they do. You cannot help your customers to lower their anxiety if you do not remember how being calm feels. To create respectful and caring relationships with your customers and coworkers, you need to create respectful and caring relationships with yourself.

A car sales career is highly demanding emotionally and intellectually. In this business, you must be able to sustain a positive attitude and hard work ethic. Your physical, spiritual, and emotional health is vital to your success in the car business and relationships with others. Reaching the calm state with yourself, where you feel appreciated, accepted, and satisfied with what you do is fundamental to your work-life balance. What do you do to stay physically, spiritually, and emotionally healthy?

_____

_____

_____

_____

_____

_____

_____

When you are able to achieve physical, spiritual, and emotional balance, customers, family, and coworkers will see your calmness. They will be drawn to it. This calmness will help you achieve satisfaction and bring you results you were looking for.

What do you wish to add or do different for your physical health?

_____

_____

_____

_____

_____

_____

What do you wish to add or do different for your spiritual health?

_____

_____

_____

_____

_____

_____

What do you wish to add or do different for your emotional health?

_____

_____

_____

_____

_____

_____

It is much harder to take care of yourself than to sell a car. It will not be easy and it requires a lot of work. Success does not come easily but that's what makes it rewarding.

Surround yourself with successful people in the car business and avoid people who discourage you and bring you down. Successful people are not afraid to share their tips for success, while people who are failing in what they do are afraid. Find a mentor who will keep you on a path to success. Find a friend who will hold you accountable. You can reach any goal that you set for yourself.

> "SUCCESS DOES NOT COME EASILY BUT THAT'S WHAT MAKES IT REWARDING."

Chapter 13

CALM-DRIVEN CUSTOMER SATISFACTION INDEX (CSI)

When customers like and trust a salesperson, they send them referrals and give 100% on a customer satisfaction survey. As a result, a salesperson and dealership make money. When customers feel disrespected, they make sure no one will come to see that salesperson and give a low score on a customer satisfaction survey. As a result, a salesperson and the dealership lose money.

Disrespect is the number one reason for customers to give a low score on a survey. Disrespect comes in many forms. Customers may feel disrespected by the way sales professionals looked at or spoke to them, by the way the negotiation process was handled, or statements that they learned were untrue. No matter what sales professionals did or how the negotiation process was handled, the most important part is how the customer interpreted the situation and their place in that situation. A feeling of disrespect can be triggered by many reasons. Two leading factors of customers feeling disrespected are feeling they are being lied to or being discriminated against.

Trust vs. Lie

A customer that feels they been lied to will interpret this as a salesperson or manager undermining their intelligence. This is equivalent to calling someone stupid, and no one thinks they are stupid. No one.

Customers who feel they have been lied to will feel played and violated. This leads them to feeling insecure with a salesperson and dealership, leading to broken trust. If the situation is not corrected, these feelings could easily escalate into feelings of stress and anxiety, making customers actively look for self-protection. If feelings of mistrust and anxiety are not defused, they will be expressed in a customer satisfaction survey, punishing the salesperson and dealership financially.

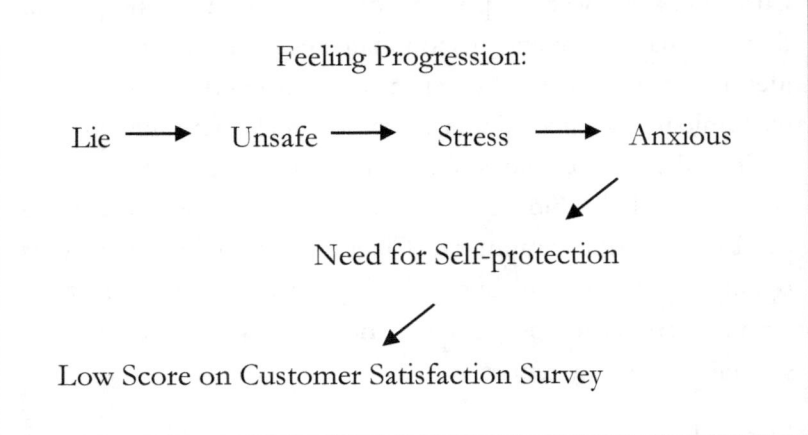

Customers feel much safer with sales professionals they trust. Trust comes with respect and a high customer satisfaction survey score. Earning customers' trust is not an easy task. Shared interest and the ability to keep a calm state through the sales process will improve trust and communication between sales professionals and buyers. Most customers will not trust you even after they take their new car home. The goal is not to make a customer believe everything you say. The goal is to assure customers that you did not lie to them.

Respect for Diversity

The second leading factor for customers feeling disrespected is being discriminated against. The law prohibits discrimination on the basis of race, color, age, ethnicity, socio-economic status, disability, gender, health status, religion, national origin, or sexual orientation. Respect for diversity includes these and many more expressions of diversity, such as height, hair color, tattoos, dress style, or intelligence.

Customers are aware of possible discrimination. A salesperson does not have to openly discriminate against a customer's identity or expression of diversity for customers to feel discriminated against. When customers feel discriminated against, their anxiety goes up. Their natural responses to anxiety, like fight, hide, run, freeze, blame, and lie increase and can lead to serious arguments. Customers who feel less safe to openly express their feelings of being discriminated against would express their negative experience on a customer satisfaction survey report.

Dealerships, politics, and culture recruit us to be bias-free. Unfortunately, it is not possible. If you are pro-something, it means you are against something else. For example, if you hold highly valued religious beliefs, you could find yourself taking a stand against marriage equality. If you value love of all sexual identities and expressions, you could find yourself against some religious beliefs.

Finding diversity balance is not easy. This does not mean that we should disrespect people's diversity. It means that we all should respect each other's diversity without judgment, understanding that we are all different. The secret to respect of other people's diversity is to accept your own biases against their identity or expression of diversity, and find your own way to understand and accept different points of view without disrespect.

> "TWO LEADING FACTORS OF CUSTOMERS FEELING DISRESPECTED ARE FEELING OF BEING LIED TO AND BEING DISCRIMINATED AGAINST."

ABOUT THE AUTHORS

SHAHEED KHAN

A top car salesperson for the last ten years with over 7500 names in his client base, Shaheed Khan is a co-owner, trainer, and Calm-Driven sales coach at Corporation Clinic, Inc.

Born in Cambridge, England, Shaheed grow up in the streets of Trinidad and Tobago. At age 9, he became homeless and started living on his own. This did not stop Shaheed from attending college in Jamaica and becoming the Masters of Society of sales and leasing for Toyota Motor Corporation (TMC) and Southeast Toyota (SET), selling 500 cars every year.

Today, Shaheed Khan shares his powerful story and inspires and educates car salespeople all over the United States to become productive, passionate, and successful in the car business.

KATIA TIKHONRAVOVA

The founder and president of Corporation Clinic, Inc., Katia Tikhonravova is completing her master's in the field of marriage and family therapy at Nova Southeastern University. She is also founder and president of The Equality Club, Inc., where she is applying her knowledge and energy to promote equality of youth, women, and men in various communities. In addition to being an international speaker, she is serving on the election committee for the Broward Association for Marriage and Family Therapy (BAMFT).

Katia was born in the Siberian town of Tomsk in Russia. Her passion for art and design guided her to a degree in architecture from Tomsk State University of Architecture and Building. She participated in National Art exhibitions in Russia. However, her desire for live conversation and business pushed her to pursue a dual degree in crisis management from the Tomsk Polytechnic University.

She decided to move to the United States on her own at 20 years-old and began her career in sales and management. Katia Tikhonravova is a Calm-Driven relational coach.

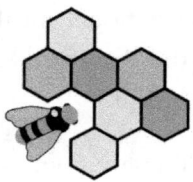

Would you like to learn more?
Visit **www.CorporationClinic.com**
www.FaceBook.com/CorporationClinic
e-mail: office@corporationclinic.com
or call: 954.253.2720 or 965.654.1656
to schedule an individual coaching session
or group training.

Notes: